Crafts for Baby

Crafts for Baby

BEAUTIFUL GIFTS AND PRACTICAL PROJECTS

Alison Jenkins

p

This is a Parragon Book

First published in 2007

Parragon

Queen Street House

4 Queen Street

Bath BA1 1HE, UK

ISBN: 978-1-4054-8785-6

Printed in China

CREATED AND PRODUCED BY THE BRIDGEWATER BOOK COMPANY LTD

PHOTOGRAPHY: *Simon Punter*

STYLIST: *Isabel de Cordova*

MODELS: *Tabitha Kitch, Finlay Warner and Kazuo Williams*

Contents

Introduction 6

For the nursery 14

Crib quilt 16

Lampshade 18

Wirework initials 20

Keepsake memory box 22

Pocket tidy 24

Cosy blanket 26

Cushions 28

Elephant bookends 30

Playroom projects 32

Soft play blocks 34

Mobile 36

Pull-along Patch 38

Floor mat 40

Teddy 42

Raggedy Ann doll 44

Cot/buggy decoration 46

Cloth book 48

Clothes 50

Dress 52

Beach robe 54

Cardigan 56

Felt bootees 58

Hat 60

Baby's first mittens 62

Trousers/dungarees 64

Fleece coat 66

Practical for parents 68

Padded hanger and drawstring bag 70

Storage bucket 72

Changing bag 74

Laundry bag 76

Changing mat 78

Nappy dispenser 80

Bib 82

Hooded towel and wash mitt 84

Templates 86

Index 96

Introduction

Getting started

A new baby – what a joy! Everyone looks forward to the arrival of a new member of the family, but for a new parent those anxious months before the birth can seem like a lifetime. During pregnancy the 'nesting' instinct is extremely strong. Apart from the obvious task of preparing the nursery for the new baby, you may find yourself compulsively reorganizing the kitchen cupboards or rearranging the furniture. This book shows you how to put your excess energies to a more productive and creative use. Try to make the most of this time because when the baby arrives there won't be enough hours in the day.

crafts for baby

★ The four sections of this book contain 32 step-by-step projects to make gifts that range from practical to decorative, from clothes to toys. Some are very simple indeed, such as the lampshade or mobile, and will take only an hour or two to complete. Others, like the beautiful crib quilt, require a little more time and effort.

You may want to create items for your own baby or perhaps make a thoughtful token or useful gift for a friend or relative. A handmade present will always be special because of the thought and time that you put into choosing and making the gift. A present made by hand is personal, unique, individual and, above all, made with love – and that is priceless.

These projects cover a range of crafts and skills from sewing to woodwork – but don't worry, you don't have to be an expert craftsperson. All you need to do is follow a few simple instructions. Take your time. You could be making a future family heirloom to be treasured by your children, and perhaps for generations to come.

basic equipment

★ Most of the projects described in this book require little or no specialist equipment in order to make them. If you are interested in crafts, you may already have all the basic sewing and painting items required. Take a look at the lists in the boxes opposite to give you an idea of what you might need; only two projects require power tools other than a domestic sewing machine and a steam iron. If you do not have these (an electric drill and a jigsaw) it will be simpler and cheaper to just borrow them from a friend rather than to buy them. Equipment specific to each project is listed under 'materials'. Always check the list first and make sure you have everything you need before you begin.

POWER EQUIPMENT

★ sewing machine
★ electric drill plus assorted bits and countersinking bit
★ jigsaw plus straight cutting and scrolling blades
★ steam iron

SEWING KIT

★ fabric-cutting scissors
★ small embroidery scissors
★ paper scissors
★ scalpel
★ dressmaker's chalk
★ sewing and embroidery needles
★ pins
★ bodkin
★ safety pin
★ sewing threads
★ embroidery silks
★ tape measure
★ ruler

DECORATIVE AND CONSTRUCTIVE EQUIPMENT

★ pencil
★ ruler
★ screwdriver
★ staple gun
★ hole punch
★ paintbrushes
★ artist's paintbrushes
★ stencil brushes
★ junior hacksaw
★ filling knife
★ long-nosed pliers

MISCELLANEOUS MATERIALS

★ fabrics
★ felt
★ Bondaweb™
★ iron-on interfacing
★ craft foam
★ ribbons
★ cords
★ pattern-making paper
★ tracing paper
★ stencil acetate
★ thick card
★ emulsion paint
★ acrylic paint
★ clear acrylic varnish
★ wood filler

ADHESIVES

★ double-sided adhesive tape
★ masking tape
★ low tack masking tape
★ spray stencil adhesive
★ repositionable spray adhesive
★ tacky craft glue
★ wood glue
★ fabric adhesive

SAFETY NOTE

Sharp instruments, power tools, paints, adhesives or any other crafter's material or equipment that is likely to be harmful to babies or small children should always be used and stored safely and carefully – and well out of the reach of curious little hands! Always check that all needles and sharp tools are removed from the product before giving it to a child.

preparation

★ All 32 projects are clearly explained in six steps and most have pattern templates or diagrams you can trace or copy. You will them find at the end of the book. Some of the patterns will need to be enlarged on a photocopier. All the patterns and templates have cutting and colour/fabric indications to help you. All fabric measurements are assumed to have been cut from material that is a minimum of 1.5 m (59 in) in width. Always be sure to copy any design, guide or construction lines carefully onto your patterns before you begin to cut out your material pieces. Colours and materials used are suggestions, feel free to choose your own.

Basic sewing skills

plain seams

★ Plain seams are used throughout this book where it is necessary to join two pieces of fabric together. Small projects can be hand stitched but we advise you to use a sewing machine for speed and effectiveness. Most of the projects list the seam allowance to be used, where it is not specified the seam should be 1.5 cm (⅝ in).

① Place the fabrics with the right sides together, pin or tack the seam securely, then stitch 1.5 cm (⅝ in) from the raw edge.

② Neaten the raw edges as directed but otherwise use a zigzag machine stitch if necessary, and then press the seam open using a steam iron.

hems

★ A hem is a double fold along the edge of a fabric piece used to neaten a raw edge. Measure and fold the hem according to the measurements given, then stitch close to the first folded edge.

① Fold once along the raw edge, pin or tack in place, then fold a second time to enclose the raw edge.

② Stitch close to the first fold.

casings

★ A casing is a channel stitched through two layers of fabric to take a drawstring or piece of elastic. Casings can either run along the edge of the fabric and look like a hem or be positioned a little way down from the edge, to give a short, frill effect above the casing.

① This casing is simply a double hem, secured with a single line of stitching along the edge of the fabric.

② The second casing is made by working a double line of stitching positioned a little way down from the edge of the fabric. You will see that the initial hem is wider and can be a single fold of fabric.

③ Once the casing is stitched, unpick a few stitches in the seam that lies across the casing. Attach a safety pin to the end of the elastic or drawstring and thread it through the casing.

gathering

★ Gathering stitches are used to reduce the width of a large piece of fabric so that it fits a smaller one, usually to create shaping or as a design feature.

① Work a row of hand running stitches across the area to be gathered, or use the largest sewing machine straight stitch. Secure one end and leave the other long.

② Pull the gathering thread so that the fabric draws together. When it is the correct size, pin or tack and then stitch to the smaller piece, matching the raw edges.

curves, corners and points

★ When making fabric shapes it is often necessary to turn the item through to the right side. If the shape has corners, points or curved seams, you need to trim or clip the seam allowance so that the fabric lies flat and neat on the right side.

① For a corner or sharp point, snip diagonally across the seam allowance before turning the item – this reduces the thickness of the seam allowance inside.

② For a curved seam, clip out little 'v' shapes at intervals along the raw edge, so that the seam allowance will lie flat on the inside.

bias binding

★ Bias bindings are a neat and decorative way of finishing a raw edge, and especially useful if the edge is a tight or small curve where a normal hem would be difficult to fold.

① Bias strips are cut in parallel diagonal lines across the fabric. For most projects the strips are 4 cm (1½ in) wide.

② The strips are combined to make one piece. Place the strips with right sides together matching the diagonal edge, then machine stitch taking a 6 mm (¼ in) seam allowance. Press the seam open.

topstitching

★ After a shape or item is complete or has been turned through to the right side and pressed, topstitching can be used as a decorative detail or to keep the finished seam flat. Simply machine stitch close to the edge of the double fabric once, or sometimes twice. You can use matching sewing thread or a contrasting colour.

③ For an internal corner, for example on heart or flower shapes, you must clip right into the seam allowance to the stitching line, as shown.

③ Working from the right side, stitch the binding along the raw edge of the fabric with right sides together. Fold a narrow hem along the remaining raw edge.

④ On the wrong side, wrap the binding around the raw edge and slip stitch the fold to the original stitching line.

Surface decoration

embroidery stitches

★ Simple embroidery stitches are used throughout the book to neaten raw edges and add decorative touches and details. The following diagrams show how to do cross-stitch, blanket stitch, running stitch, backstitch and satin stitch.

BLANKET STITCH

CROSS-STITCH

BACKSTITCH

SATIN STITCH

RUNNING STITCH

appliqué

★ Appliqué is the name given to the application of a decorative fabric shape to another fabric. This can be done by hand or machine.

MACHINE APPLIQUÉ

❶ Machine appliqué makes use of a clever double-sided adhesive material called Bondaweb™. First trace your shape onto the paper side of a piece of Bondaweb™, then iron it to the wrong side of the fabric to be appliquéd.

❷ Cut out the shape carefully then peel away the Bondaweb™ backing paper.

❸ Use a warm iron to fuse the cut-out shape to the base fabric, then use a small machine zigzag stitch around the edge of the shape to secure.

HAND APPLIQUÉ

❶ Cut out the shape to be applied (most templates have a 6-mm (¼-in) seam allowance included), then tack in position on the base fabric.

❷ Using the tip of your needle, tuck the raw edge under the shape, then neatly slip stitch the resulting fold to the base fabric.

Woodworking

stencilling

★ Using a stencil is an extremely quick and easy method of applying repeated motifs in paint, to fabric or any other flat surface. Simply trace the stencil design onto paper then fix the paper to a sheet of thick card. Tape a sheet of clear acetate film over the design, then, on a safe cutting surface, carefully cut out the shapes following the pencil lines using a scalpel or sharp craft knife. Remove the stencil and apply some spray stencil adhesive to the back. Place the stencil in position on the fabric. Pour some acrylic paint onto a saucer or palette, then take up a little paint on the bristles of a stencil brush. Wipe away the excess paint on a piece of kitchen paper then apply the paint to the fabric through the stencil using a dabbing motion. Several colours can be used on the same stencil but you must use a different brush for each colour.

power tools

★ Using power tools can be a little daunting – but never fear, they are quite safe when used correctly. Be sure to wear a protective mask when drilling or cutting as these craft activities create a lot of dust.

USING A JIGSAW

Use a power jigsaw for making cuts in sheet materials such as plywood. Begin by placing your material on a workbench, then hold the jigsaw firmly and start the motor. Slowly guide the blade along the cutting line. Always work slowly and carefully. Use a straight cutting blade for straight cuts and a scrolling blade for curves.

USING A DRILL

An electric drill makes light work of hole-making in all sorts of materials – simply use the correct diameter bit to match the hole required. Always make sure that the drill bit is inserted into the drill correctly and keep the drill straight.

pilot holes and countersinking

★ Before inserting a screw into a piece of wood, you must first make a 'pilot hole'. This is a drilled hole a little smaller than the diameter of the screw itself. The pilot hole acts as a guide for the screw and prevents the wood splitting. The pilot hole may then be 'countersunk' using a countersinking drill bit. This makes a shallow recess at the entrance to the pilot hole so the screw head can lie flush with the surrounding surface. You can hide the hole with wood filler and paint.

gluing

★ Wood and plywood should always be joined using wood glue. Apply a bead of glue to the surfaces to be joined and then press both together firmly. Wipe away any excess glue that may seep out from the join using a damp cloth, then allow the join to dry.

preparing plywood for painting

★ Plywood is a versatile material made from thin layers of wood compressed together to make a thick sheet. When plywood is cut, gaps or 'voids' are sometimes seen along the cut edge. These are simply air gaps between the layers, but they must be repaired with a wood filler before painting. Apply the filler using a filling knife, smoothing out the surface with the blade. When the filler is dry, use sandpaper to rub the repaired area smooth. This filling method can also be used to repair any surface damage.

painting

★ Painting is a relatively easy job, but to get the best results always rely on adequate preparation beforehand. When applying paint onto a bare wood, plywood or MDF surface a suitable primer must be applied first. This prepares the surface and creates a good key for the topcoat. Allow the primer to dry completely before applying the topcoat, and if necessary sand down the primed surface and apply a second coat. Remember to wipe away all dust particles using a damp cloth after sanding.

For the nursery

Crib quilt

What better way to spend those last weeks before your baby arrives than making a traditional quilt? The larger pieces are machine stitched together, but the heart motifs and general quilting are done by hand. Spend time and care over the hand stitching to make this quilt an item that will last a lifetime.

materials

- pencil and tracing paper
- sewing kit (see page 9) and sewing machine
- 20 cm (8 in) each of 6 or more red and white gingham, striped, spotted, and patterned fabrics
- 50 cm (20 in) plain red fabric
- 10 cm (4 in) white and red polka-dot fabric
- 1 m (39½ in) lightweight wadding
- 1 m (39½ in) red gingham fabric for backing
- steam iron

NOTE *When choosing your fabrics, try to include three light-toned and three darker-toned patterns that work well together and with plain white and red. All templates include a 6-mm (¼-in) seam allowance.*

TEMPLATES P87

1 Trace the heart motif, strap (the rectangular strip between the large squares) and corner square templates provided on page 87 onto tracing paper. You will also need a pattern for the large square patches, which are simply 17.5-cm (7-in) squares.

2 To begin, you need to cut out the following:
- 12 large squares: 6 light-toned pattern and 6 dark-toned red and white patterned or striped fabric
- 12 heart-shaped motifs: 6 light-toned pattern and 6 dark-toned fabrics
- 17 rectangular straps from plain red fabric
- 10 corner squares from red polka dot fabric (try to keep a dot in the centre of the square)
- approximately 4 m (158 in) of 4-cm (1½-in) wide bias strips from plain red fabric
- approximately 4 m (158 in) of 4-cm (1½-in) wide straight strips from red and white striped fabric
- 1-m x 75-cm (39½-in x 29½-in) rectangle of polyester wadding
- 1-m x 75-cm (39½-in x 29½-in) rectangle of red gingham for backing

3 Take the large squares and the heart shapes and experiment with different pattern combinations – you will find that some work better than others. When you are satisfied, tack each heart into position about 1.5 cm (⅝ in) from the raw edge. Turn the raw edge of the fabric heart to the wrong side using the tip

of your needle and slip stitch the fold in place neatly. (See hand appliqué, step 2 on page 12.)

4 Lay the large squares on the floor, 4 x 3 squares to make a rectangle, alternating light and dark shades. Place a red strap between each square and along the outside edges. Now place a small square at each corner. Stitch all the pieces together one row at a time, taking a 6-mm (¼-in) seam allowance, then stitch the rows together to make the quilt top. This may take a little while, but it is worth taking time to make sure that all the corners are neat and matching. Press the seams open at each stage.

5 Stitch a red-and-white striped strip to each long side of the quilt top first, then across the short ends. Now sandwich the wadding between the quilt top and the gingham backing fabric. Tack the three layers together vertically and horizontally at approximately 10-cm (4-in) intervals. Now work a small running stitch through all the layers along the main seam lines. Try to keep the stitches small and regular, and wear a thimble to save your fingertip!

6 When the quilting is complete, remove all tacking stitches and trim the edge of the quilt top neatly. Join the plain red bias strips together to form one continuous length then apply the binding to the outside edge (see page 11). You could trim the corners of the quilt to a softly rounded shape before binding to make it easier.

Lampshade

A very simple decorative project that can be completed in an hour or two, this underwater marine theme is calm and soothing. However, you could adapt the idea to make a brighter shade using other colours. You can also use it as a pendant shade; the soft shadows cast around the nursery will hopefully capture your tiny baby's attention. The fish shapes are very easy to cut – perhaps an older child could help.

materials

- pencil and tracing paper
- scissors
- tape measure
- pale blue drum-shaped lampshade (plus base if required)
- large pale blue polypropylene sheet
- white craft foam sheet
- hole punch
- double-sided adhesive pads
- double-sided adhesive tape

TEMPLATES P88

① To begin, trace the wave and fish templates provided on page 88 onto tracing paper, then cut out carefully. Indicate the eye position on each fish shape with a small circle or pencil dot.

② Measure the exact circumference of your shade then add approximately 2 cm (¾ in) for an overlap. Extend the wave shape to make a new template that matches this measurement.

③ Lay the wave template onto the polypropylene sheet and trace around the edge using a sharp pencil. Repeat this to make two wave strips, but you can use more if your shade is larger. Now cut along the pencil lines carefully using scissors.

④ Cut out small and large fish shapes from the white craft foam sheet in the same way. The number will depend on the size of your shade, but use approximately 10 large fish and 30 smaller ones. Remember to indicate the eye on each fish, then make a small hole using the hole punch at that point.

⑤ Take the double-sided adhesive pads and fix three or four at equally spaced intervals on one side of each wave. Peel off the backing paper and fix around the shade. Use a tab of double-sided adhesive tape to secure the overlap. Do likewise with the other or subsequent strips.

⑥ Stick an adhesive pad to the back of each fish shape. You may trim the pad to fit if it is too large for the small shapes. Fix the fish to the waves, alternating large and groups of small shapes.

Wirework initials

These delicate wirework initials make an unusual christening gift or a thoughtful token to mark the arrival of a new baby, and can easily be sent through the post as a greeting. However, you could make the gift a little more special by making a drawstring bag and gift box to hold it. Copy the heart-shaped template first, then practise drawing a nice cursive initial in the centre. Alternatively, you could make a decorative pattern instead of an initial if you prefer.

materials

- pencil and tracing paper
- masking tape
- piece of stiff card
- 2-mm (¹/₁₆-in) diameter coloured craft wire
- long-nosed pliers
- fine jewellery wire
- 70 cm (27¹/₂ in) pink organza ribbon for the gift pouch
- 20-cm x 40-cm (8-in x 16-in) strip white organza
- sewing kit (see page 9) and sewing machine
- steam iron
- safety pin
- 50 cm (20 in) pink organza ribbon
- gift box (optional)

TEMPLATE P88

① Trace the template provided on page 88 onto tracing paper, then enlarge to the required size. Tape the template to a piece of stiff card to use as a guide when bending the wire. The aim is to form the heart shape and wavy border from a single length of wire. It is best to practise bending and curling the wire on a short spare piece before starting the project.

② Begin with the tight scroll shape that lies at the top centre of the heart, then bend the basic heart shape. Place the wire shape on the template outlines as you work to make sure the shape is correct.

③ Next, bend the small wavy border that surrounds the central shape. This is a little fiddly but will become easier as you work. Snip off the wire neatly when the shape is complete. Next, take a shorter length of wire and bend it to match the initial you have drawn. Make sure that it fits neatly inside the heart shape.

④ To keep the wires in place they must be bound together with fine jewellery wire. Begin with the loop at the top centre and work around the shape, binding each section in turn. When the heart shape is secure, place the initial in position and bind it to the frame securely.

⑤ Take the longer length of organza ribbon and tie it into a pretty bow and hanging loop around the scroll at the top of the heart shape. Trim the ends of the ribbon into neat fishtail points.

⑥ For the gift pouch, simply fold the organza strip in half, then stitch both sides together. Fold a narrow hem along the top raw edge, then fold a larger 5-cm (2-in) hem and press. Now stitch a 1.5-cm (⁵/₈-in) casing (see page 10) about 5 cm (2 in) from the top edge. Turn the pouch to the right side and press. Unpick a few stitches in the seam between the stitching lines of the casing on one side, then using a safety pin thread the casing with ribbon. Place the wire heart inside, gather up the pouch and tie the ribbon in a bow. Place inside a gift box if desired.

Keepsake memory box

Where do you keep all those precious tiny items that remind you of your baby's first days, months or years? The hospital wristband, lock of baby hair, pictures of the newborn, the birth certificate, or first tiny bootees, gloves and clothes. A memory box is the answer. The soft pastel exterior conceals a colourful fabric lining, complete with co-ordinating storage items such as a photo album, scrapbook and note book, to record all those 'firsts' and family moments that you don't want to forget.

materials

- box
- wood filler
- medium grade sandpaper
- white wood or multi-surface primer
- paintbrush
- pale yellow satinwood paint
- sewing kit (see page 9)
- 1 m (39½ in) pink fabric with a bold pattern
- steam iron
- extra tacky craft adhesive
- 3 m (118 in) white satin ribbon
- scrapbooks, photo albums, little boxes
- 50 cm (20 in) toning fabric with a smaller pattern
- double-sided adhesive tape
- staple gun

① Make sure the exterior and interior surfaces of the box are clean and dry. Repair any exterior surface imperfections with wood filler, then, when dry, rub the area down with medium grade sandpaper. Wipe away all dust particles using a damp cloth. Your box is now ready for painting.

② To ensure a good finished result, a coat of primer should be applied to bare wooden or MDF surfaces. When the primer is dry, apply two (or more if necessary) coats of satinwood paint, allowing appropriate drying time in between applications. Make sure to paint the edges of the box and lid, but leave the inside unpainted.

③ While the paint dries, cut out the pink fabric to line the interior. Cut one strip to fit around the sides, allowing for a 2.5-cm (1-in) hem at the top edge and a 1.5-cm (⅝-in) overlap at the side and lower edges, then a piece to fit the base, allowing a 2.5-cm (1-in) hem on all four sides.

④ Cut all the linings to size and fold and press the hems neatly. Apply adhesive to the sides of the box then carefully press the lining fabric into position, matching the pressed hem to the top edge of the box and smoothing the raw edge overlap into the corners at the base. Snip into the overlap at each corner so that the fabric lies flat. Now glue the base lining into position.

⑤ The lid is lined in the same way, but stitch a pocket to the main part before gluing. Use a ribbon tie to keep the pocket closed. To accessorize the memory box, gather together a collection of scrapbooks, albums, little boxes, etc., and cover them in a co-ordinating fabric secured by tabs of double-sided adhesive tape. You can add to the memory box as the years go by.

⑥ Finally, cut a strip of the lining fabric approximately 6 cm x 12 cm (2½ in x 4½ in). This will form the loop with which to lift the box lid. Apply some adhesive down the centre of the strip on the wrong side. Now fold both long edges to meet in the centre and press firmly down onto the wet adhesive. When the adhesive is dry fold the strip in half, then fix the end to the inside of the lid using a staple gun.

NOTE *Fabric quantities are calculated for a box approximately 30 cm x 30 cm x 60 cm (12 in x 12 in x 24 in). Allow more or less fabric for a larger or smaller box. You can use one made from plywood, solid wood or MDF. Many craft companies produce 'blank' shapes for decorative purposes, or you could use one from your own childhood, or an inexpensive 'antique' from a charity shop.*

Pocket tidy

This pretty pocket tidy with its jolly spotted fabric and colourful pockets is an ideal storage device for all those small bits and pieces required for your baby's well-being and comfort. Hang it at a suitable height so it's within easy reach when you are seated and feeding or nursing your baby.

materials

- pencil and tracing paper
- sewing kit (see page 9) and sewing machine
- 30 cm (12 in) each of four toning plain coloured cotton fabrics
- 1.8 m (71 in) spotted fabric
- steam iron
- 50 cm (20 in) of 6-mm (¼-in) wide elastic
- 2 x 1-m (39½-in) lengths of 12-mm (½-in) diameter wooden dowel
- hacksaw
- 3 m (118 in) cord

NOTE *Template and fabric measurements include a 1.5-cm (⅝-in) seam allowance.*

⬤ TEMPLATE P95

❶ Trace the flap template provided on page 95 onto tracing paper, then enlarge to the size required. Now cut out the following fabric pieces:

- 2 flap pieces in each of the four plain fabrics
- 2 x 55-cm x 85-cm (21½-in x 33½-in) rectangles of spotted fabric for the base and backing
- 1 x 27-cm x 85-cm (10½-in x 33½-in) rectangle of spotted fabric for the top pockets
- 1 x 27-cm (10½-in) strip of spotted fabric across the whole width of the fabric for the lower pockets
- 1 x 10-cm x 85-cm (4-in x 33½-in) strip for the dowel channel at the lower edge
- 5 x 15-cm x 8-cm (6-in x 3-in) rectangles of spotted fabric for the hanging tabs

❷ Stitch the flap pieces together in pairs around the outside edge, trim across the seam allowance at each point (see page 11), then turn through to the right side and press. Fold and stitch a 2-cm (¾-in) double hem across one long edge of both pocket strips. Press a single 1-cm (½-in) hem at the lower edge of the shorter strip.

❸ Lay the flaps side by side in a row with the points upwards. Now place the hemmed edge of the shorter pocket strip on top to cover the raw edge of each flap. Pin and stitch the flaps to the strip. The flaps will fold down to cover the stitching lines. Position the pocket strip on the base rectangle 5 cm (2 in) down from the top raw edge, then stitch the pocket divisions vertically.

❹ Divide the remaining strip pocket into quarters and mark the divisions with pins. Thread elastic through the hem along the top edge using a safety pin. Pull the elastic quite tight so as to gather up the central two quarters only. The gathering should correspond with the width of the middle two flap pockets. Now hand stitch through the hem and the elastic inside to secure. Pin the pocket strip in place on the backing, then pleat up the remaining fabric at each end to fit. Machine stitch the vertical pocket divisions as in step 3.

❺ Fold and machine stitch a double hem down each side of the tidy and along the top edge. Take the remaining narrow fabric strip and stitch it to the lower edge with right sides facing. Fold in the seam allowance on the three raw edges then fold the strip around the lower raw edge of the tidy, rather like a wide binding. Slip stitch the long folded edge to the backing fabric on the wrong side. Cut a length of dowel, using a hacksaw, to fit across the tidy then insert it into the channel.

❻ Fold each tab in half lengthwise with right sides facing, then stitch the long edges together taking a 1.5-cm (⅝-in) seam allowance. Turn each through to the right side and press. Fold each tab in half then stitch the short raw edges to the wrong side of the top hem of the tidy. Slot the dowel through the tabs and tie the cord to both ends. Knot the cord securely forming a hanging loop as shown in the picture.

Cosy blanket

A monogram or even a simple shape like a heart or a teddy can transform a plain comfort blanket into something quite special and personal. This blanket uses cream and pale blue fleece to make a reversible, double-thickness blanket. The initial is simply blanket stitched in place, cream on blue and blue on cream. Both layers are securely held together around the outside edge with a row of regular blanket stitches. You may make a blanket to fit your baby's crib, or perhaps you'd like to make a smaller one for nursing or to fit inside the buggy or Moses blanket.

materials

- sewing kit (see page 9)
- 1 cream fleece blanket
- 1 pale blue fleece blanket
- small plate or saucer
- pencil or dressmaker's chalk
- plain paper
- 5 skeins cream embroidery silk
- 1 skein blue embroidery silk

① First trim your fabric pieces to the size required. Place the cream fleece on top of the blue, measure carefully and then cut through both layers at the same time. The cream layer will be trimmed a little smaller at a later stage.

② Use a small plate or saucer as a template to cut the corners into soft curves. Place the saucer/plate next to the right-angled corner and draw around the edge using a pencil or dressmaker's chalk. Cut carefully along the curved line and discard the waste.

③ The size of the monogram depends largely on the size of the blanket. Experiment a little with a paper cut-out before you decide. For the template, draw a large letter on a piece of paper then smooth out and round off all the sharp edges and corners to make a softly rounded squat shape. The fleece fabric is not suitable for tight curves and sharp corners.

④ Cut out one blue and one cream letter and place each in one corner of the opposite coloured fleece. Tack the letter in place, then work a neat blanket stitch using cream or blue embroidery silk around the edges (see page 12).

⑤ Now place the cream fleece on top of the blue. Tack both layers together approximately 2.5 cm (1 in) from the outside edges. Using sharp scissors trim the cream layer about 1.5 cm (5/8 in) smaller than the blue layer underneath.

⑥ Fold the edge of the blue fleece over the raw edge of the cream layer to form a mock binding then tack in place. Now work a regular blanket stitch around the outside using a cream coloured embroidery silk (see page 12).

Cushions

If you love the seaside, you'll adore these three cushions. The size you choose is up to you – make them tiny for a chair or larger for a day bed – simply enlarge the template as required. The basic construction and background sections are machine stitched while the smaller details are appliquéd by hand.

materials

- sewing kit (see page 9) and sewing machine
- 1 m (39½ in) blue chambray fabric for the sky and cushion backs
- 30 cm (12 in) plain blue fabric for the sea
- steam iron
- pencil and tracing paper
- 30 cm (12 in) beige mottled pattern fabric for the sand
- palm-sized scraps of red, white, beige, yellow and assorted striped fabric
- scraps of red gingham ribbon
- 3 x 50-cm (20-in) cushion pads

NOTE *Use spare scraps of fabric for small details. Each template represents the size of your cushion plus 1.5-cm (5/8-in) seam allowance on all 4 sides.*

TEMPLATES P89

① For each cushion cut the following pieces:
- 2 x 3-cm x 33-cm (21-in x 13-in) rectangles from blue chambray for the cushion backs
- 53-cm x 28-cm (21-in x 11-in) rectangle from blue chambray for the sky
- 53-cm x 28-cm (21-in x 11-in) rectangle from plain blue fabric for the sea

Stitch the sky and sea pieces with right sides facing, taking a 1.5-cm (5/8-in) seam allowance, then press the seam open. This forms the background for each cushion front.

② Trace the cushion templates provided on page 89 onto tracing paper, then enlarge to the required size. You will need to retrace each of the details (beach huts, sun, sandcastles, lighthouse, boat, etc.) of the design in turn, then add a 6-mm (1/4-in) seam allowance to the edges. Use the picture as a guide and cut each section in turn from the appropriate fabric.

③ Tack the 'sand' in place on each of the three background squares, then turn the wavy raw edge under using the tip of your needle. Slip stitch the fold neatly to the background (see hand appliqué, step 2 on page 12). Next, appliqué the beach huts, the sun, the sandcastles and then the basic lighthouse shape in the same way.

④ Small details like the boat, lighthouse base and top can be tricky to apply. However, they give

an extremely professional result and it is worth taking your time.

⑤ To complete the design, add some small machine-stitched details. Adjust your sewing machine to a narrow satin stitch setting and work three vertical windows down the centre of the lighthouse using red thread. Trim the gingham ribbon to form two tiny pointed flags and satin stitch (see page 12) them to the sandcastles using a beige thread. Now remove all tacking threads.

⑥ Fold and stitch a narrow double hem across one long edge of each of the cushion backs. Place two cushion backs onto each cushion front with right sides facing. Match the raw edges around the outside and overlap the hemmed edges in the centre. Machine stitch around the outside taking a 1.5-cm (5/8-inch) seam allowance. Trim diagonally across the seam allowance at each corner (see page 11), then turn the cushion through to the right side and press.

Elephant bookends

Yes, you are seeing pink elephants! These jolly fellows will hold a row of small books safely on a bookshelf or table top. The height of each bookend measures approximately 15 cm (6 in), but you can always enlarge the template a little more than the recommended percentage to make a bigger Jumbo for larger and heavier books – but remember you'll have to enlarge the base, too.

materials

- pencil and tracing paper
- 1-cm (¹/₂-in) thick plywood (or small offcuts from the wood yard)
- jigsaw plus blades (straight cutting blade and scrolling blade)
- medium grade sandpaper
- wood filler
- electric drill plus bits, and countersink bit
- white primer
- paintbrush
- wood glue
- 6 x 2.5-cm (1-in) long wood screws
- pink satinwood paint

TEMPLATES P87

① Trace the elephant templates provided on page 87 onto tracing paper, then enlarge to the appropriate size as directed. Lay the templates on the plywood and draw around the edge using a sharp pencil. You will need two elephant shapes and four ears. Also mark out four rectangles measuring 15 cm x 7.5 cm (6 in x 3 in) for the bases.

② Place the plywood on a workbench or safe and steady cutting surface, then cut along the pencil lines with a jigsaw. Use a straight cutting blade for the base rectangles and a scrolling blade to cut the curved elephant and ear pieces.

③ You may find that the cut edges are a little splintered. If so, simply rub smooth using medium grade sandpaper. Repair any voids and surface unevenness (see painting on page 13).

④ Using a fine drill bit and an electric drill, make a small hole where indicated to represent the elephant's eye. Now apply a coat of white primer to all pieces and allow to dry. Examine the surfaces and sand away any unevenness. Apply a second coat of primer and resand. Wipe away all dust particles using a damp cloth in preparation for the pink topcoat.

⑤ Glue the base rectangles together to form two right angles. Allow the glue to set a little then drill two pilot holes through the right-angle join. Countersink each drill hole, insert a wood screw to secure the join, then fill the screw hole and sand smooth (see page 13).

⑥ Glue the ears to each elephant and then glue the elephants' feet to each base. Allow the glue to dry then screw the feet to the bases from underneath, making a pilot hole first then countersinking the screw hole as before. Apply two coats of pink paint, allowing each coat to dry before applying the next.

Playroom projects

Soft play blocks

Your baby will enjoy playing with these soft blocks on many different levels. Building, balancing and construction will be learned at a later stage, but certainly hugging, chewing and throwing skills will develop really quickly here. The star-shape motifs are securely held in place with double-sided adhesive material and a zigzag machine stitch.

materials

- pencil and tracing paper
- sewing kit (see page 9) and sewing machine
- 6 x 20-cm (8-in) squares in assorted pink and blue plain and patterned fabrics per block

- 20 cm (8 in) Bondaweb™ double-sided adhesive material
- polyester toy filling

NOTE *Block templates include a 1.5-cm (⁵/₈-in) seam allowance, stars need none.*

TEMPLATES P95

① Trace the templates provided on page 95 onto tracing paper then enlarge to the appropriate size as directed. You will need six different coloured fabric squares and two star shapes for each block. Use the picture as a guide to colour and pattern arrangement or design your own. For cutting out the stars, see machine appliqué on page 12.

② Place your fabric pieces together in groups of six. Next, peel off the backing paper from each of the star shapes and apply to the centre of two squares from each pile. Adjust your sewing machine to a zigzag stitch setting and carefully stitch around the edges of each star shape.

③ To assemble each block, take the four pieces that will form the sides, then pin and machine stitch them together to form a cylinder with right sides facing, taking a seam allowance of 1.5 cm (⁵/₈ in). Remember to leave a small gap in the stitching at the centre of one of the seams so that you can turn the block to the right side.

④ Stitch the top and bottom squares to the side piece, taking care to keep the corners neat and unpuckered. You will need to snip a few stitches at each end of the side seams so that the top corners lie flat.

⑤ Turn each block through to the right side. Use your finger or the tip of a pair of scissors to gently ease out the corners from inside the shape, taking care not to burst through the seam.

⑥ Stuff each block with toy filling so it feels quite firm but not too solid – your baby should be able to grasp the block quite easily. Slip stitch the small opening in the seam using a matching sewing thread.

Mobile

A mobile is always a popular choice for a nursery – use these pretty pastel colours or choose ones to tone with the nursery colour scheme. This mobile uses simple concentric circle and flower shapes that move and spin to create a focus for your little one's gaze – and probably your own! Craft foam is easy to use and cut, but coloured paper or thin card would work well too. Each element of the mobile is a pair of shapes stuck together; the fine thread is sandwiched securely between the layers.

materials

- pencil and tracing paper
- scissors
- 1 x 42-cm x 30-cm (16½-in x 11½-in) piece each pink, green and blue craft foam
- double-sided adhesive tape
- masking tape
- beading thread
- long-nosed pliers
- wire coat hanger
- yellow spray paint
- 50 cm (19½ in) yellow satin ribbon
- large needle and thread

TEMPLATES P87

① Trace the flower, circle and disc templates provided on page 87 onto tracing paper, then enlarge to the required size as directed. Cut out the paper templates then transfer the outlines to the coloured craft foam, following the colour cutting guide carefully.

② It is a good idea to set out all the larger circle, disc and flower pieces in the appropriate pairs on your work surface, using the picture as a guide to the colour combinations and shape groupings. Allow a space of about 10 cm (4 in) between each flower and circle or disc group. At this stage, keep all the smallest central discs to one side.

③ When you are satisfied with your arrangement you may begin to string the separate elements together. It's best to start with the central group. Remove the top shape of each pair, then apply strips of double-sided tape down the centre of each piece. When you cut it you will need to allow for the holes in the centre of each shape. Now remove the backing papers.

④ Use a tab of masking tape to fix the end of the beading thread to your work surface about 20 cm (8 in) above the top circle. Lay the thread onto the tape checking the length of the thread between each shape. You can now replace the top shapes, sandwiching the thread inside securely. Do likewise with the other two groups.

⑤ Use small tabs of double-sided tape to secure the small central discs to the centre of each flower and circle. Using pliers, cut a 25-cm (10-in) length of wire from a coat hanger then bend a tiny loop at each end. Apply a coat of yellow spray paint to the wire and allow to dry.

⑥ Place a tab of double-sided tape to the centre of the ribbon length and remove the backing paper. Place the centre of the wire onto the tape. Fold the ribbon around the wire and squeeze the adhesive tape together to hold the wire securely. Use a large needle to stitch the central motif group to the ribbon, then tie the other two groups to the small loop at each end of the wire. Tie the ends of the ribbon in a knot and hang the mobile in a suitable place out of reach of children.

Pull-along Patch

Woof woof! It's easier than you think to make a cute little canine on wheels to guard your nursery and entertain a toddler. Patch's body is just a few flat plywood shapes glued together, and the wheels are actually small wooden drawer knobs fixed to short dowel axles. If you feel particularly artistic, why not paint your pulling Patch toy to match the family pet?

materials

- pencil and tracing paper
- sheet 1.5-cm (⅝-in) thick plywood
- jigsaw with scrolling blade
- medium grade sandpaper
- natural coloured wood filler
- wood glue
- white primer
- paintbrush
- white satinwood paint
- black, brown and red acrylic paints
- small artist's paintbrush
- small stencil brush
- electric drill with 6-mm (¼-in) and 8-mm (⅜-in) bits
- 4 small wooden drawer knobs
- 2 x 8-cm (3-in) lengths of 6-mm (¼-in) diameter wooden dowel
- 20 cm (8 in) red satin ribbon
- 1 m (39½ in) black satin ribbon

TEMPLATES P88

① Trace the templates provided on page 88 onto tracing paper then enlarge to the size as directed. Lay the templates on the plywood and trace around the edge using a sharp pencil. You will need to cut one body, two front legs and two hind legs. All other details are painted on later.

② Place the plywood on a work bench or safe and steady cutting surface, then cut along the pencil lines with a jigsaw fitted with a scrolling blade. This blade will allow you to cut around tight curves with ease.

③ You may find that the cut edges are a little splintered. If so, simply rub smooth using a medium grade sandpaper. Prepare the plywood as directed on page 13.

④ Glue the legs to the body shape and allow to dry completely. Next, apply a coat of white primer to both sides and edges of the shape and allow to dry. Examine the surfaces and sand away any unevenness. Apply a second coat of primer and resand. Wipe away all dust particles using a damp cloth in preparation for one or two coats of white satinwood paint. Apply the paint.

⑤ Refer to the picture and the template design lines then apply the eyes, ears and dark coloured patches to the dog's body with black and brown acrylic paint. Acrylic paint is the best for this type of surface decoration because it dries quickly. Paint the eyes, ears and basic patches using a small artist's paint brush, then soften the edges of the patches using a small stencil brush. Paint the four wooden knobs red.

⑥ For the wheels simply drill an 8-mm (⅜-in) hole through the body and leg shapes, making sure that the holes are low enough down for the bottom of the wheels to be below the bottom of the legs so that the toy can move freely. Then drill a 1-cm (½-in) deep 6-mm (¼-in) diameter hole in the centre of the flat underside of each wooden knob. Glue a knob to one end of each dowel and allow the glue to dry. Pass the dowels through the pre-drilled holes in the body shape then glue on the remaining two knobs. Make a collar from the red ribbon and finally attach a black ribbon lead.

Floor mat

'Quack quack, croak croak!' Jumping frogs and fluffy ducks form a pretty border to this very easy-to-make floor mat. It's just a rectangle of heavyweight natural canvas painted with leftover household emulsion – what could be simpler? Use it in the nursery, or take it out into the garden to play counting games or to aid with storytelling in fine weather. The surface is sealed with clear varnish so any accidental spills or dirty footprints can be easily wiped away using a damp cloth.

materials

- pencil and tracing paper
- low tack masking tape
- sheet of thick card
- sheets of stencil acetate
- scalpel
- heavyweight natural canvas
- ruler
- scissors
- mini sponge roller
- white matt emulsion paint
- green and yellow emulsion paint
- spray stencil adhesive
- yellow, green and red acrylic paint
- stencil brush
- clear satin-finish acrylic varnish
- paintbrush
- tacky craft glue

TEMPLATES P88

① Trace the frog and duck stencil templates provided on page 88 onto tracing paper then enlarge to the appropriate size as directed. Copy each design onto a separate sheet of paper. Use tabs of masking tape to fix the tracings to a sheet of thick card, then fix a sheet of stencil acetate over each one. Carefully cut out the stencil using a scalpel (see page 13).

② Draw and cut out a rectangle of canvas using the diagram measurements as a guide. Be sure to use a ruler and measure carefully to ensure that the edges are straight and the corners true right angles. Using a mini sponge roller apply two or three coats of white matt emulsion paint to the canvas, allowing each coat to dry before applying the next.

③ When the white paint is dry, use a ruler and very faint pencil lines to indicate the border areas and coloured central bands, following the measurements on the diagram. Next use long strips of low tack tape to mask off the border and central areas ready for the next painting stage.

④ Apply green and yellow emulsion paint to the masked off areas using a mini sponge roller. Be sure not to overload the roller as this may cause paint to bleed under the masking tape. Remove all tape strips when the paint is dry.

⑤ Refer to 'stencilling' on page 13 to guide you through the next stage. Make a frog stencil using green acrylic paint at each corner and at the centre point of each side. Position yellow ducks on each side of the frog, reversing the stencil to make a symmetrical pattern. Remember to add a touch of red paint to accentuate the beak and webbed feet.

⑥ When all the decorative paintwork is dry, apply a coat of clear acrylic varnish to seal the surface. Allow plenty of time for the varnish to dry then turn the mat over to the other side. Draw two pencil lines, 2.5 cm (1 in) and 1.5 cm (5/8 in) from the outer edge of the mat. Snip across each corner diagonally from the raw edge to meet the first line, then apply glue to the marked hem area. Fold over the raw edge to meet the second pencil line – making sure the corners mitre neatly.

Teddy

Many adults have very fond memories of a favourite toy from childhood. Every baby deserves their very own huggable teddy bear to love, and maybe keep on loving till they grow up. This fluffy bear is filled with the softest natural fibres and is fully washable.

materials

- pencil and tracing paper
- sewing kit (see page 9) and sewing machine
- 30 cm (12 in) short pile, washable fur fabric with a brown suede underside
- natural, washable toy filling

- soft pencil or dressmaker's chalk
- brown embroidery thread
- ribbon for teddy's bow tie

NOTE *Templates include a 6-mm (¹/₄-in) seam allowance.*

TEMPLATES PP92–93

① Trace the teddy pattern templates provided on pages 92–93 onto tracing paper then enlarge to the appropriate size as directed. Cut out the pattern pieces and then cut out carefully in fur fabric.

② Fold each leg and arm piece in half with right sides facing, taking a 6-mm (¹/₄-in) seam allowance, then stitch the long seams together. Stitch the sole pieces to the bottom of the legs, placing the reverse sides of the soles to the fronts of the legs. Turn each arm and leg piece to the right side and stuff with toy filling. Be sure not to overfill the pieces. Now machine stitch or tack across the opening so the filling does not spill out.

③ Take the face piece and fold in half. Stitch the long seam together (this runs from the nose to the neck). Then stitch across the short seam that will form the nose. Stitch the face to one body piece and the back of the head to the remaining body piece.

④ Place the back of the head and body flat on your work surface with the right side facing you, then tack the top of each leg to the lower edge. Tack the top of each arm then stitch the ears in place. Remember to make a small pleat in each ear piece as indicated on the pattern.

⑤ Fold the arms and legs inwards then place the front body and face on top. Tack the two pieces together leaving a gap along the lower body edge so that you can turn teddy to the right side. Turn the shape through to the right side now, then stuff the body and head with toy filling. Carefully slip stitch to close the opening.

⑥ Using the picture as a guide, mark the eye, nose and mouth position using a soft pencil or dressmaker's chalk. Thread a bodkin with brown embroidery silk then use long satin stitches (see page 12) to make the features.

Raggedy Ann doll

Many girls adore their dolls, taking them everywhere until they become very raggedy indeed! This doll measures approximately 35 cm (14 in) in length, but you could scale the pattern up to make a larger, almost life-size doll for an older child.

materials

- pencil and tracing paper
- sewing kit (see page 9) and sewing machine
- 20 cm (8 in) white cotton fabric for head and hands
- 20 cm (8 in) pink-and-white striped cotton fabric for body and limbs
- scrap of plain pink cotton fabric for shoes
- toy filling
- broderie anglaise trim
- soft pencil or dressmaker's chalk
- blue, white and red embroidery silk for face
- 30 cm (12 in) white cotton piqué fabric for dress
- brown chunky-weight knitting wool for hair
- 1 m (39½ in) pink gingham ribbon

NOTE *Templates include a 6-mm (¹/₄-in) seam allowance, aside from neck and armholes.*

TEMPLATES P92

① Trace the doll and dress templates provided on page 92 onto tracing paper then enlarge to the appropriate size as directed. Following the instructions, cut out all the pieces from white, striped and pink cotton fabrics. As the pieces are quite small, it is important to mark out and cut carefully and accurately.

② With right sides together, stitch the hands to the arms and the shoes to the legs, then stitch both head and body pieces together. Fold each leg and arm piece in half with right sides facing and stitch the long seams together. Then stitch across the short curved seam at the hand/shoe end. Turn each piece to the right side and stuff with toy filling – be sure not to overfill the pieces. Now machine stitch or tack across the opening so the filling does not spill out.

③ Place one head and body piece flat on your work surface with the right side facing you, then tack the top of each leg to the lower edge. Tack the top of each arm to the side of the body.

④ Fold the arms and legs inwards then place the front body and face on top. Tack the two pieces together leaving a gap at the lower body edge to turn the doll shape to the right side. Turn through to the right side now, then stuff the body and head with toy filling. Carefully slipstitch the opening closed.

⑤ Stitch the side seams of the dress bodice together, apply a narrow binding to the neck and armhole edges (see 'binding' page 11), then join both shoulder seams. Stitch the centre back skirt seam together, stitch a narrow double hem across the lower edge, then apply a strip of broderie anglaise trim. Dress Raggedy Ann and hand stitch the centre back seam securely. Tie a gingham ribbon around her waist.

⑥ Using the picture as a guide, mark the eye, nose and mouth position using a soft pencil or dressmaker's chalk. Use blue, white and red embroidery silk to work the features. Hand stitch loops of chunky brown knitting yarn to the head to form Ann's hair and fringe. Make two long plaits to complete her hairstyle then finish with two pretty gingham ribbon bows.

Cot/buggy decoration

Folk-art heart and bird motifs combine to form a stylish cot or buggy decoration that has that special 'homespun' feel. Why not hide a squeaker in one of the padded hearts as a surprise for curious little fingers to discover? This decoration uses just five shapes, but if you have time on your hands you could make lots more and extend it for use across a window in the nursery.

materials

- pencil and tracing paper
- sewing kit (see page 9) and sewing machine
- 10 cm (4 in) each of three toning small print cotton fabrics
- scraps of pale blue felt and pink felt for wings and tiny heart motif
- polyester toy filling
- squeakers (optional)
- tacky fabric adhesive
- blue embroidery thread
- 2-m (79-in) length x 1-cm (1/2-in) wide blue striped ribbon
- 2-m (79-in) length x 6-mm (1/4-in) wide blue gingham ribbon

NOTE *Bird and heart templates include a 6-mm (1/4-inch) seam allowance. No allowance is needed for the wings and small heart.*

① Trace the heart and bird templates provided on page 89 onto tracing paper, then enlarge to the appropriate size as directed. Cut out two fabric pieces for each shape, plus one wing in felt for each bird and one small heart for the central shape.

② Place the fabric pieces together in pairs with the right sides facing. Stitch around the outer edge taking a 6-mm (1/4-in) seam allowance. Remember to leave a small gap in the stitching so that you can turn the shape through to the right side.

③ Turn each shape to the right side and stuff quite firmly with toy filling. You may at this stage insert a little squeaker in each one. Carefully slipstitch the opening closed.

TEMPLATES P89

④ Use a spot of tacky fabric adhesive to secure the wings to each of the birds and a tiny heart to the central heart shape. When the glue is dry, stitch the wings in place with a small row of backstitches (see page 12), and the heart with one cross stitch (see page 12).

⑤ Cut the wider ribbon in half and lay it out flat on your work surface. Place the padded shapes on top allowing about a 5-cm (2-in) gap between each one. Pin the shapes to the ribbon, then hand stitch securely in place using double sewing thread and back stitches. Place the second strip of ribbon on top of the first just to hide the securing stitches.

⑥ To complete the decoration, cut the narrow gingham ribbon into six 20-cm (8-in) lengths. Tie each short length to the ribbon at each end and between the padded shapes – this secures the wider ribbon lengths and draws the shapes together a little. Secure each knot with a few overstitches, then tie each into a bow. Trim all ribbon ends into pretty points.

Cloth book

Small children and babies love to look at different shapes, colours and patterns, even before they can read. A soft cloth book is the ideal starting point for young learners. This book is made entirely from cotton fabrics and pretty scraps rescued from the workbox and is completely washable – keep it in your changing bag to entertain your baby any time, anywhere!

materials

- pencil and tracing paper
- sewing kit (see page 9) and sewing machine
- 20 cm (8 in) each red, yellow, green, blue and lilac gingham fabrics
- 50 cm (19½ in) white cotton fabric
- scraps of plain cotton fabric to tone with gingham
- 30 cm (12 in) Bondaweb™
- steam iron

NOTE *Templates include a 1.5-cm (⅝-inch) seam allowance. No allowance is needed for the shapes.*

TEMPLATES P86

① Trace the flower, fruit and tree templates on page 86 onto tracing paper to make 12 shapes. Then enlarge to the appropriate size as directed. Follow the instructions for machine appliqué on page 12, then cut out each piece in a different coloured gingham or plain fabric. Make sure you leave enough gingham to edge the pages. This is an ideal opportunity to use up all the little scraps in your sewing bag.

② Cut out six white cotton rectangles following the dimensions on the diagram, then fuse the shapes to each of the pages (see page 12). Each shape must be secured to the fabric 'page' using a zigzag machine stitch.

③ Cut the remaining gingham fabric into 4-cm (1½-in) wide straight strips to use as binding for each page. Stitch a different coloured gingham edge to each page, first along each short side then across the top and bottom edges. Press the seams flat.

④ Place the pages right sides together in three pairs. Stitch together around the outside edge taking a 1.5-cm (⅝-in) seam allowance. Leave a small gap in the stitching at the lower edge so that you can turn the page to the right side.

⑤ Trim diagonally across the seam allowance at each corner, then turn each piece to the right side and press. Slip stitch the opening in the seam at the lower edge of the page.

⑥ Place the pages one on top of the other, choosing your favourite image to be the 'front cover'. Tack through all the layers at the centre to secure. Now machine stitch the book together. Make sure to work three or four rows of machine stitching so that the pages will not come undone.

Clothes

Dress

What could be nicer for a baby girl than a pure white cotton piqué dress? This classic little number would be perfect for an afternoon stroll in the buggy or even at a party. The design is very simple to make and has a delicate daisy trim to accentuate the hems, neckline and bodice seam.

materials

- pencil and tracing paper
- 1 m (39½ in) white cotton piqué
- 20 cm (8 in) lightweight iron-on interfacing
- steam iron
- sewing kit (see page 9) and sewing machine
- 3 small white buttons
- 3 m (118 in) daisy trim

NOTE *Template pieces include a 1.5-cm (⁵/₈-in) seam allowance and the skirt has a 5-cm (2-in) hem. The size is suitable for a 3- to 6-month-old baby.*

TEMPLATES P90

① Trace the dress patterns provided on page 90 onto tracing paper, then enlarge to the appropriate size as directed. Cut out all the pieces from white cotton, then cut out the front and back neckline facings again from a lightweight iron-on interfacing. Fuse the interfacing to the wrong side of the facings using a steam iron.

② Stitch the shoulder seams of the bodice and neckline facings together, then press the seams open. Apply the facing to the neckline with right sides together. Machine stitch along the centre back edges and around the neckline. Trim the seam allowance down to about half and then clip into the curved neckline edges (see page 11).

③ Work a large gathering stitch between the marked dots on each sleeve head. Pull up the gathering stitches so that the sleeve fits into the armhole. Stitch each sleeve in place, then join the bodice side seam and sleeve seam in one. Fold and stitch a 1-cm (½-in) double hem around the lower edge of each sleeve.

④ Join the skirt seam from the hemline to 5 cm (2 in) from the top edge, then press the seam open. Fold and stitch a 2.5-cm (1-in) double hem around the lower edge. Now work a large gathering stitch around the top edge and gather up the skirt to fit the bodice seam. Pin and stitch the skirt to the bodice with right sides facing, keeping the gathers even all the way around.

⑤ Fold and press a 1.5-cm (⁵/₈-in) turning along the centre back bodice/skirt opening. Slip stitch the centre back neck facing edges neatly to the turnings on the inside. Work three button holes on the centre back overlap where indicated, then sew three buttons on the underlap to correspond.

⑥ Machine stitch the daisy trim to the stitching line of the skirt and sleeve hem, then around the neckline and along the bodice seam line.

Beach robe

Utilize a large bath sheet to make this cuddly and absorbent beach robe for your baby. All parents know how difficult it is to keep their baby still when they're trying to dry them after a dip in the bath or the sea. With this garment it's easy – just pop it over their heads and they can dry themselves as they run or crawl around. It's easily washable too, so all that sand and ice cream present no problem at all!

materials

- pencil and tracing paper
- one large patterned bath sheet
- sewing kit (see page 9) and sewing machine
- steam iron

NOTE *Templates include a 1.5-cm (⁵/₈-in) seam allowance. Neaten all raw edges with a machine zigzag stitch to prevent fraying. The size is for a 6- to 9-month-old baby.*

🌀 TEMPLATES P93

① Trace the patterns provided on page 93 onto tracing paper, then enlarge to the appropriate size as directed. Cut out all pattern pieces from the bath sheet as indicated. Remember to make use of the woven hems of the towel for the edge of the hood, lower edge of robe and sleeve hems.

② Join the front and back shoulder seams together with right sides facing. Neaten the seam allowances then press the seam open.

③ Fold the hood piece in half with right sides together then stitch the centre back seam together. Stitch the neck seam to the neckline of the robe, taking care to overlap the front edges at the centre front neckline point.

④ Fold and stitch a narrow hem along both side edges of the pocket piece, then tack a narrow hem along the upper and lower edges. Lay the robe out flat and pin the pocket in place just below the front neck in the centre of the robe. Machine stitch the pocket in place along the upper and lower edges.

⑤ Pin the centre of each sleeve head to the shoulder seam, then stitch the sleeves in place. Press both seams open.

⑥ Join the side and sleeve seams in one, then neaten the seam allowances with a machine zigzag stitch and press the seams open.

Cardigan

Cashmere and silk, what a luxurious combination – only the best for your baby! These natural fibres feel so soft and gentle against the skin that your baby will be extremely comfortable, and so smart too. This basic, T-shaped garment is very simply constructed, and finished with unusual velvet ribbon toggles.

materials

- pencil and tracing paper
- sewing kit (see page 9) and sewing machine
- a long cashmere and silk mix scarf
- 50 cm (19½ in) striped silk fabric for the lining (this could also be a large head scarf)
- steam iron

- 1-m (39½-in) length of 1.5-cm (⁵⁄₈-in) wide velvet ribbon in a toning shade for toggle fastenings

NOTE *Sleeve and the sides and armholes of the front and back templates include a 1-cm (½-in) seam allowance. The size is for a 3-month-old baby.*

TEMPLATES P91

1 Trace the patterns provided on page 91 onto tracing paper, then enlarge to the appropriate size as directed. Cut out each piece from the knitted fabric and the striped silk lining fabric. Cut approximately 1.5 m (59 in) of 4-cm (1½-in) wide bias strips from the striped fabric for the bindings (see bias bindings on page 11).

2 Start by stitching the shoulder seams of the cardigan together then press the seams open. Stitch the sleeve to the armhole position matching the centre sleeve head to the shoulder seam, then join the sleeve and side seams in one. Make up the cardigan lining in exactly the same way.

3 Press all seams open – you do not need to neaten the seam allowances. Turn the lining inside out then place it inside the cardigan. Tack the wrist edges, lower hem, centre front and neckline edges together.

4 Cut 4 x 8-cm (3-in) lengths and 4 x 10-cm (4-in) lengths of velvet ribbon for the toggle and loop fastenings. Fold the four shorter pieces in half and tack the raw ends to the right centre front edge, spacing evenly. The loop should lie flat and at this stage it will point towards the garment front.

5 For the toggle part of the fastening, simply fold the longer ribbon pieces in half and make a knot close to the folded end. Tack the raw edge to the left front edge to correspond with the loops on the other side.

6 Join the striped bias strips together to make one continuous strip and then apply the binding to the raw edges of the sleeves, the lower edge and front/neckline edge (see page 11).

Felt bootees

Make the cutest pair of felt bootees as an unusual gift for a friend or relative with a new baby.
The two-tone pink and blue colour scheme would suit a boy or a girl, and the tiny heart-shape
motif on the sole is a little surprise that will make the recipient smile.

TEMPLATES P94

materials

- pencil and tracing paper
- sewing kit (see page 9) and sewing machine
- 2 large sheets of felt, one pink and one blue
- 1 m (39½ in) pink silk cord
- pinking shears

NOTE *Templates include a 6-mm (¼-in) seam allowance. The size is for a newborn baby.*

① Trace the patterns provided on page 94 onto tracing paper, then enlarge to the appropriate size as directed. Cut out the bootee pieces in pink and blue felt as indicated, plus a little pink heart motif for each bootee sole.

② Place a pink upper and a blue upper together and tack around the outside edges. Machine stitch the pieces together along the dotted line. Now trim the curved edge of the ankle cuff using pinking shears.

③ Using a hole punch, carefully make three holes through both felt layers in the position indicated on the pattern. Make sure that the diameter is slightly larger than the diameter of your silk cord.

④ Fold each upper in half with the pink layer on the inside. Stitch the centre front seam together to the dot indicated on the template, taking a 6-mm (¼-in) seam allowance, then trim the seam allowance neatly using pinking shears.

⑤ Position a heart shape on each sole and tack in place. Adjust your sewing machine to a small zigzag setting and carefully stitch around the outside edge of the shape to secure.

⑥ Tack and machine stitch the sole to each bootee then pink the seam allowance neatly. Cut the pink silk cord in half and thread though the lacing holes on each bootee. Tie the ends in pretty bows. Trim all the long thread ends carefully, to a maximum length of 1 cm (½ in).

Hat

'If you want to get ahead, get a hat!' The greatest percentage of body heat is lost through the top of the head, and it is very important that a baby does not get cold on those chilly days out in the park. This little fleece number is made in a trice and the tassel on the top and the hand-worked running stitch detail add that special touch.

materials

- pencil and tracing paper
- sewing kit (see page 9) and sewing machine
- 30 cm (12 in) blue fleece fabric
- 30 cm (12 in) white fleece fabric
- pale blue and white embroidery silk

NOTE *Templates include a 1.5-cm (⅝-in) seam allowance. The size is for a 3-month-old baby.*

TEMPLATES P92

1 Trace the patterns provided on page 92 onto tracing paper, then enlarge to the appropriate size as directed. Cut out one piece in blue and one in white, placing the pattern piece to the fold, plus a tassel piece in each colour.

2 Place the tassel pieces one on top of the other. Stitch together along the dotted line as indicated, then make parallel cuts from the outer edge towards the stitching line approximately 6 mm (¼ in) apart to form a fringe. Roll the tassel up tightly from the wider end and towards the shank, then secure the roll at the base with several hand-worked overstitches.

3 Begin with the white hat piece. Stitch the two short crown seams together then tack the shank of the tassel to the point where the seams meet. Now join the longer centre back/crown seam in one. All the seams should meet neatly at the top of the crown.

4 Make the blue lining in the same way, then place it inside the white hat piece, ensuring that the right sides are facing and that the lower edges match. Tack the lower seams together, then machine stitch. Remember to leave a small gap in the stitching so that you can turn the hat to the right side.

5 Turn the hat through to the right side and then slip stitch over the gap in the stitching to complete the basic construction.

6 Using a bodkin and blue and white embroidery threads, work a large but even running stitch around the lower edge of the hat (see page 12). This will help to keep the edge flat.

Baby's first mittens

Newborn babies have beautiful, tiny hands but often have extremely sharp fingernails, so they can easily scratch their delicate skin. Make these mittens from the softest fleece and line them with a pretty spotted lawn fabric to keep your baby warm and his or her skin protected.

materials

- pencil and tracing paper
- sewing kit (see page 9) and sewing machine
- 15 cm (6 in) ivory fleece fabric
- 15 cm (6 in) white and pink spotted cotton lawn fabric

- 30-cm (12-in) of 6-mm (¹⁄₄-in) wide elastic
- 50 cm (19¹⁄₂ in) narrow satin ribbon in cream or pink

NOTE *Templates include a 6-mm (¹⁄₄-in) seam allowance. The size is for a newborn baby.*

TEMPLATE P92

① Trace the mitten pattern provided on page 92 onto tracing paper, then enlarge to the appropriate size as directed. Cut out two pieces in fleece and two in the spotted lawn fabric.

② Fold each piece in half with right sides together. Stitch the outer shaped edges together taking a 6-mm (¹⁄₄-in) seam allowance.

③ Turn both lining pieces to the right side. Now slip the spotted linings into the fleece mitten pieces. The right side of the lining should face the right side of the fleece mitten. Stitch the top edge together leaving a small gap so you can turn the mitten through to the right side.

④ Turn the mittens through to the right side now, then slip stitch the small gap closed. Tuck the spotted lining down inside each fleece mitten, and tack close to the seam around the top edge.

⑤ This next part will be a little tricky as the mittens are so small. Stitch a 1-cm (¹⁄₂-in) wide casing (see casings on page 10) about 2 cm (³⁄₄ in) from the top edge on both mittens. Unpick a few stitches in the seam between the casing stitching lines and thread a short piece of elastic through using a safety pin. Pull up the elastic a little, so that the wrist of each mitten is gathered but loose enough to allow the baby's hand to fit through. Stitch the ends of the elastic together.

⑥ Cut the ribbon in half and stitch the centre of each piece to the casing on the underside of each mitten. Tie the ribbon in a pretty bow then trim the ends to neat points. Trim all the long thread ends carefully, to a maximum length of 1 cm (¹⁄₄ in).

Trousers/dungarees

Perfect for napping, playing, or simply crawling around the floor, these cute dungarees are quick and easy to make – in fact, you could make several pairs to suit all seasons. The inside leg seam is fastened with Velcro™ for easy nappy changing – what could be better?

TEMPLATES P94

materials

- pencil and tracing paper
- sewing kit (see page 9) and sewing machine
- 80 cm (31½ in) blue star-patterned cotton fabric
- 30 cm (12 in) white cotton fabric for lining
- steam iron
- 10 small circular Velcro™ fasteners

NOTE *Templates have a 1.5-cm (⅝-in) seam allowance included. The size is for a 6- to 9-month-old baby.*

① Trace the patterns provided on page 94 onto tracing paper, then enlarge to the appropriate size as directed. Cut out the pattern pieces from the blue star fabric as indicated, then cut the front and back bodice pieces again from plain white cotton lining fabric. Cut approximately 2 m (79 in) of 4-cm (1½-in) wide bias strips of blue fabric for the bindings (see bias binding on page 11).

② Place the bodice pieces and the white linings together in pairs and tack together around the outside edges. Now join the front and back crotch seams together with right sides facing.

③ Work a large gathering stitch along the top edge of the front and back leg pieces. Pull up the gathering stitches a little to the leg pieces to fit the lower edge of the front and back bodice. Machine stitch in place.

④ Apply the binding to the armhole, neckline and fastening tab edges of the front and back bodice. Fold and machine stitch a 1-cm (½-in) double hem across both ankle edges then apply bias binding to each inside leg seam.

⑤ Place the front and back of the dungarees together with right sides facing, then join both side seams from ankle edge to the base of the fastening tab. Press the seams open and then turn to the right side. Topstitch the opening.

⑥ Separate the Velcro™ fasteners and stitch the loop part to the lining on the underlap and the hook part to the overlap of the inside leg opening, the side tabs and the shoulder straps.

Fleece coat

Your baby will be so comfy and warm from head to toe in this full-length coat, she'll never want to take it off — whether it's an afternoon snooze or snuggling in the buggy while out strolling. The toggles are made from fleece too, so there are no hard edges to disturb your baby's sleep.

materials

- pencil and tracing paper
- sewing kit (see page 9) and sewing machine
- 1 m (39½ in) each pale pink and dark pink fleece fabric

NOTE *Templates have a 1.5-cm (⁵⁄₈-in) seam allowance included. The size is for a 3- to 6-month-old baby.*

TEMPLATES P95

1 Trace the patterns provided on page 95 onto tracing paper, then enlarge to the appropriate size as directed. Cut out all pattern pieces in pale pink and dark pink fleece fabric.

2 Begin with the dark pink pieces. Join the shoulder seams together with right sides facing, then stitch each sleeve to the armhole position, matching the centre sleeve head with the shoulder seam. Join the sleeve and side seam in one. Make the light pink fleece lining in exactly the same way.

3 Take the hood pieces and fold in half with right sides together. Join the centre back seam first, then stitch across the short seam to give the hood a square shape. Stitch the lower edge of the hood to the neckline seam of the coat and lining.

4 Place the dark and light pink toggle pieces together in pairs and stitch together along the dotted line. Roll up the toggle from the wide end towards the shank. Secure the roll at the base with several hand stitches. Fold each loop piece in half, then topstitch close to the fold. Tack the toggles to the right front edge of the coat and the loops to the left.

5 Place the lining inside the outer coat with right sides together. Stitch the front edge and hood seam together then turn the coat through to the right side. Topstitch the front edge and hood seam about 1.5 cm (⁵⁄₈ in) in from the edge. Slip stitch the hem of the coat and lining together around the wrist edge.

6 To complete the coat, stitch both layers together around the lower edge about 5 cm (2 in) up from the raw edge. Make a series of parallel cuts into the fleece fabric from the raw edge towards the stitching line to form a fringe.

Practical
for parents

Padded hanger and drawstring bag

Padded hangers for special outfits look so much nicer and keep clothes looking special for longer. Choose a wooden, child-sized hanger for this project – you could even recycle an old one that you already have. And why not make a tiny little drawstring bag to match the hanger, just to keep matching accessories, like socks and ribbons, safe.

materials

- pencil and tracing paper
- sewing kit (see page 9) and sewing machine
- 50 cm (19½ in) blue embroidered gingham fabric
- 20 cm (8 in) plain green fabric
- 30 cm (12 in) wadding
- wooden child-sized coat hanger
- steam iron
- pale blue embroidery silk

NOTE *Bag measurements include a 1.5-cm (⅝-in) seam allowance.*

TEMPLATE P95

1 Trace the pattern for the coat hanger provided on page 95 onto tracing paper then enlarge to the appropriate size as directed. Cut out one hanger cover and one bag piece of 28 cm x 11 cm (11 in x 4½ in) from gingham fabric, and one bag piece of 28 cm x 13 cm (11 in x 5 in) from plain green fabric. Cut 4-cm (1½-in) wide bias strips from the gingham to be used later for the hook covers, bows and drawstrings.

2 Cut a rectangle of wadding large enough to wrap around the hanger. Pierce a small hole in the centre of the wadding and pass the hook through. Wrap the edges of the wadding snugly around the wooden hanger and tack securely in place.

3 For the hook cover, cut a 10-cm (4-in) length of bias strip from gingham fabric, fold it in half, then stitch across the short end and up the side edge. Turn the cover to the right side and slip it over the hook. Stitch the raw end of the hook cover to the wadding at the base of the hook.

4 Pierce a small hole through the centre of the fabric hanger cover then pass the hook through. Wrap the fabric around the padded hanger and

fold in the raw edges at each end and along the lower edge. Slip stitch the folds together neatly.

5 Join both bag pieces together and press the seam open. Work a row of cross stitches on the seam line using blue embroidery silk (see page 12). Fold the bag in half with right sides together then stitch across the bottom and side edges. Fold a 2.5-cm (1-in) hem around the top edge, then stitch 1.5 cm (⅝ in) from the fold to form a casing. Unpick a few stitches in the seam between the stitching lines of the casing.

6 Cut two 25-cm (10-in) lengths of bias binding from the gingham. Fold each in half and stitch across both short ends. Then stitch across the long edge leaving a small gap in the stitching at the centre. Turn the strips to the right side through the gap to form the tie and the drawstring then slip stitch the gap closed. Now stitch the tie to the base of the hook and then tie in a bow. Thread the drawstring through the casing at the top of the bag, then tie the ends in a knot.

Storage bucket

Storage with a difference! Any household containing a small baby quickly becomes overwhelmed with bottles, tubes, lotions and potions, powders and other vital bits and pieces of baby toiletry. Use a galvanized bucket as an unusual storage item with a pretty drawstring bag inside. It's sturdy, waterproof and stylish too, for use in the bathroom, garden or even on the beach.

materials

- white primer
- paintbrush
- galvanized bucket
- green and pink spray paint or metal paint
- sewing kit (see page 9) and sewing machine
- 1 m (39½ in) pink gingham fabric
- 1 m (39½ in) green canvas
- eyelet kit
- steam iron

NOTE *Measurements include a 1.5-cm (⅝-in) seam allowance.*

① Apply a coat of white primer to the galvanized bucket and when dry apply the green and pink paint in wide bands as shown.

② Cut a circle from the pink gingham the size of the base of the bucket, then cut a rectangle from green canvas and pink gingham to fit the circumference of the top of the bucket and about twice the height. For the drawstring, cut a gingham strip 8 cm x 1 m (3 in x 39½ in). For the ties cut two strips 15 cm x 5 cm (6 in x 2 in) from gingham fabric.

③ Indicate a 4-cm (1½-in) wide casing about 8 cm (3 in) down from the top edge of the green canvas piece using dressmaker's chalk. Mark two eyelet positions at the centre of the casing then insert as per kit instructions. Fold both the canvas and lining pieces in half and stitch the side seams together. Press the seams flat.

④ Place the bag and lining together with right sides facing. Stitch together along to the upper edge. Turn to the right side and tuck the lining inside the bag. Press the seam flat then topstitch close to the upper edge. Stitch a 4-cm (1½-in) wide casing where indicated, making sure that the eyelets are correctly positioned.

⑤ Pin the bag and lining layers together along the lower raw edge then work a large gathering stitch close to the edge. Pull up the gathering stitches so that the bag fits the circular fabric base. Stitch the bag to the base, placing the right side of the base to the inside of the bag, so the raw edge will not be seen inside the bag.

⑥ For the ties and drawstring, fold the long and short strips in half with right sides facing, then stitch across each short end and along the side seam leaving a gap at the centre. Turn the strips to the right side and slip stitch over the gaps, then press the strips. Stitch one short tie to each side of the bucket, and thread the long drawstring through the casing. Place the bag inside the bucket and secure the ties to the handle on each side.

Changing bag

Every new parent is surprised by how much 'stuff' they need to carry around with them when they have a small baby to look after. This voluminous canvas bag is large enough to hold just about everything you could possibly need and more. It has long carry handles and three extra pockets on the outside for small items. What's more, the bag folds completely flat for easy storage when not in use.

materials

- pencil and paper
- scissors
- 1 m (39½ in) turquoise canvas cotton fabric
- 1 m (39½ in) print cotton fabric for lining
- sewing kit (see page 9) and sewing machine
- steam iron
- scrap Velcro™ for tab

NOTE *Templates include a 1.5-cm (⅝-in) seam allowance.*

TEMPLATES P94

① Make paper patterns for the bag, pocket, straps and tabs following the diagrams given on page 94. Cut out two bag pieces, one pocket and two straps from the canvas and the print fabric, plus one print fabric tab.

② Place the pocket and lining pieces together with right sides facing then stitch across the top edge. Press the seam open then refold the pocket so the wrong sides are facing. Re-press the top seam then topstitch close to the edge (see topstitching on page 11). Place the pocket onto the bag front, matching the lower stepped edges. Stitch vertical pocket divisions where indicated on the pattern.

③ Place the two bag pieces together with right sides facing. Stitch the side seams together then stitch the seam that runs across the lower edge. Pin the side seams to the lower seam, then stitch the edges together. This forms the square-shaped base of the bag.

④ Make the lining up in exactly the same way, but leave a gap in the seam that runs along the base so you can turn the bag to the right side. Place the lining inside the bag with right sides facing. Stitch both layers together around the top edge. Now turn the bag and lining to the right side through the gap in the lower lining seam. Slip stitch the gap closed.

⑤ Tuck the lining down inside the bag and press the top seam neatly. Topstitch close to the fold along the top edge. Fold the tab piece in half with right sides together then stitch down the side and across one short end. Turn it through to the right side and press, then stitch a small piece of Velcro™ to the underside at one end. Stitch the tab to the bag just inside the top of the middle pocket, then stitch on a corresponding Velcro™ fastening to the outside of the pocket under the tab.

⑥ Place both canvas straps and the lining pieces together with right sides facing, then stitch together down both long sides. Turn the straps to the right side and topstitch close to both side edges. Fold a 1.5-cm (⅝-in) hem across the short ends then pin and machine stitch the straps in place on the bag as shown in the picture.

Laundry bag

It is truly amazing how much laundry your tiny little bundle can generate in just a day! This laundry bag, with pretty three-dimensional daisies, has a huge capacity and drawstring ties for hanging on a hook inside the nursery door. It's made entirely from pure cotton, so you can pop the bag into the wash whenever it's necessary.

materials

- pencil, paper and tracing paper
- sewing kit (see page 9) and sewing machine
- 50 cm (19½ in) pink chambray fabric
- 25 cm (10 in) blue chambray fabric
- 70 cm (27½ in) white cotton fabric
- 30 cm (12 in) blue gingham fabric
- steam iron
- handful of polyester toy filling

NOTE *Bag templates include a 1.5-cm (⁵⁄₈-in) seam allowance. Flower template includes a 6-mm (¹⁄₄-in) seam allowance.*

TEMPLATE P87

1 Make paper patterns for the bag following the diagrams provided on page 87, then trace the daisy template onto tracing paper and enlarge to the appropriate size as directed. Cut out the bag pieces from pink and blue chambray, the lining from white cotton and the daisy shapes from white cotton and blue gingham. Cut approximately 1.5 m (60 in) of 4-cm (1½-in) wide bias strips, and 1.5 m (60 in) of 4-cm (1½-in) wide straight strips from blue gingham for the binding and the drawstring.

2 Place the white daisy shapes together in three pairs. Stitch together around the outside edge taking a 6-mm (¹⁄₄-in) seam allowance, remembering to leave a small gap in the stitching. Snip into the seam allowance at the corners and clip the curved edges (see page 11). Now turn the shapes through to the right side. Slip stitch the gap closed then press the shapes flat.

3 Stitch together the pink and blue chambray pieces and press the seam open. Tack the daisy shapes in place side by side along the seam on the front half of the bag. Place the gingham circles in the centre of each flower, tuck a small amount of toy filling under each circle, then tuck in the raw outside edge, tack in place and machine stitch to the bag.

4 Stitch the side and lower seams of the bag and lining together then place the lining inside the bag with the wrong sides facing. Tack the top edges together then apply the blue gingham binding to cover the raw edge (see page 11).

5 Now fold the long raw edges of the straight gingham strip to the centre and then fold in half again. Tuck in the raw edges at each short end and then machine stitch close to the edge to make the drawstring.

6 Stitch a 2-cm (³⁄₄-in) wide casing (see page 10) approximately 10 cm (4 in) down from the top edge. Unpick a few stitches in the seam that lies between the stitching lines of the casing and then thread the drawstring through using a safety pin. Tie the drawstring in a bow or knot the ends together.

Changing mat

Your baby needs changing regularly – whether you're at home or on the move. Carry this pretty roll-up changing mat over your shoulder when you and your baby are out and about. There's a pretty floral cotton print on one side and polka-dot wipe clean oilcloth on the other.

materials

- pencil and paper
- small plate or saucer
- sewing kit (see page 9) and sewing machine
- 60 cm (23½ in) blue spotted oilcloth
- 80 cm (31½ in) floral print cotton fabric to tone with the oilcloth
- steam iron

① Make a paper rectangular pattern measuring 80 cm x 50 cm (31½ in x 19¾ in). Use a small plate or saucer as a template to round off each corner. Cut out one piece in oilcloth and one in cotton fabric.

② Cut two 9-cm x 80-cm (3-in x 31½-in) strips from the floral cotton fabric for the carry handle and tie, then cut about 3 m (118 in) of 4-cm (1½-in) wide bias strips of cotton for the binding.

③ Place the cotton and oilcloth pieces together with wrong sides facing. Tack together around the outside edge. Take the carry handle strip and fold it in half lengthways. Stitch the long edges together then turn it through to the right side and press. Tack the raw ends of the handle to the long sides of the mat on the cotton side about 15 cm (6 in) down from one end so that it stretches across the mat.

④ Join the floral bias strips together to form one continuous length, then apply the binding to the outside edge of the mat (see page 11).

⑤ Take the remaining tie strip and fold it in half lengthways. Stitch across the short ends and down the long edge leaving a small gap in the stitching at the centre so that you can turn the tie to the right side. Trim diagonally across the seam allowances at each corner (see page 11), then turn the strip to the right side and press flat.

⑥ Slip stitch the gap closed, then fold the strip in half. Machine stitch the halfway point of the tie to the mat on the floral side at the centre of the short end, nearest the carry handle.

Nappy dispenser

How many nappies will you use during your baby's early years, you may wonder? Although an absolutely essential part of your babycare equipment, the plastic bag packaging is not really very pretty, is it? Why not make a little dispenser to hold your disposable nappies, or even terry nappies if folded up neatly? Think 'duffel bag' when you make this – it's simpler than it looks.

materials

- pencil and paper
- sewing kit (see page 9) and sewing machine
- 1 m (39½ in) pink spotted fabric
- eyelet kit
- steam iron
- 1 m (39½ in) white cord
- 2 circular Velcro™ fasteners
- thick card
- fabric adhesive

NOTE *Templates include a 1.5-cm (⁵/₈-in) seam allowance. Material allowances are based on a pack of newborn baby nappies.*

TEMPLATES P93

① Make a paper pattern following the diagrams provided on page 93. Cut out one bag piece, one base and a flap from the spotted fabric. Cut a rectangle of fabric about 5 cm (2 in) larger than the base all round to cover the base stiffener. Cut 50 cm (19½ in) of 4-cm (1½-in) wide bias strip for the binding.

② Apply the bias binding to the curved edge of the semi-circular opening (see page 11). Now fold a 10-cm (4-in) wide hem along the top edge. Stitch a 4-cm (1½-in) wide casing about 2.5 cm (1 in) from the top edge (see page 10). Mark eight evenly spaced eyelet hole positions along the casing and insert each one following the kit instructions.

③ Fold the flap in half with right sides together then stitch across both short sides. Turn to the right side and press, then topstitch close to three edges, leaving the raw edge free. Tack the two lower corners of the flap to the base of the semi-circular opening on both sides.

④ Stitch the rectangular base to the lower edge of the dispenser bag with right sides facing, taking care to snip into the seam allowance at each corner so that the fabric lies flat. Now turn the bag to the right side.

⑤ Cut a strip of fabric about 10 cm x 5 cm (4 in x 2 in). Fold the long raw edges to the centre then fold in half again. Fold the short ends to the centre and overlap slightly. Machine stitch through all the layers at the centre to form a fabric 'stay' for the drawstring. Thread the cord drawstring through the eyelets and through the fabric stay. Tie the ends of the cord together in a knot and tuck inside the bag out of sight.

⑥ Separate the two Velcro™ fasteners, then stitch the hook part to each corner of the flap and the loop part to the dispenser in a corresponding position. Wrap the remaining rectangle of fabric around a stiff piece of card cut to fit the dispenser base. Glue the edges of the fabric to the card on the underside. When the glue is dry, pop the stiffener into the base.

Bib

Let's face it, when it comes to feeding time, babies don't really care where the food goes – keeping clothes clean is just not a priority! Protect garments with a good old-fashioned bib. These two pretty bibs are completely washable, and the acrylic paint is permanent when dry, so the cute Scottie-dog motifs won't fade or run in the washing machine.

materials

- pencil and tracing paper
- sewing kit (see page 9)
- 40 cm (15½ in) white cotton fabric
- 30 cm (12 in) red gingham fabric
- 30 cm (12 in) black gingham fabric
- sheet of thick card
- masking tape
- stencil acetate
- spray stencil adhesive
- red and black acrylic paint
- saucer or palette
- stencil brush
- small artist's paintbrush
- 2 circular Velcro™ fastenings

TEMPLATES P89

1️⃣ Trace the patterns for the bib shape and the Scottie stencil provided on page 89 onto tracing paper, then enlarge to the appropriate size as directed. Cut two bib pieces from white cotton (you can use a double layer if the cotton is quite fine), then cut about 1 m (39½ in) of 4-cm (1½-in) wide bias binding from both the red and black gingham fabric.

2️⃣ Fix the tracing outline to a piece of thick card using tabs of masking tape and tape the acetate sheet on top. Carefully cut out the stencil using a scalpel (see stencilling, page 13).

3️⃣ Lightly coat the back of the stencil with adhesive spray then place in position on the bib. Pour some red paint onto a saucer or palette then take up a little on the stencil brush, dab off excess paint on a spare sheet of paper then apply the paint through the stencil (see page 13). Do likewise on the other bib but use black paint.

4️⃣ When the stencil work is dry, use a small artist's brush to paint in the details. Give the red Scotties a black collar and eyes, and the black Scotties red collars and eyes. You could alternate red and black Scotties on the same bib if you want to be a little more creative.

5️⃣ Join the red bias strips together to make one continuous length and the black bias strips together to make a second continuous length, then apply the red binding to the bib with black Scotties, and vice versa.

6️⃣ Separate both Velcro™ fasteners then, on each bib, stitch the loop part to the bib underlap at the neckline and the hook part to the overlap.

Hooded towel and wash mitt

A classic babycare item – once you've used one of these, you will never look back. Bathtime with a new baby is always fun for parents and little ones alike, but drying a wet wriggling baby afterwards can be easier said than done! Swaddle your baby in this fluffy hooded towel after bathing, and he or she will soon be dry. There is a matching wash mitt too, for having fun with bubbles while getting clean.

materials

- large white bath sheet
- sewing kit (see page 9) and sewing machine
- 30 cm (12 in) multi-coloured, striped cotton fabric
- small saucer

1 Lay the bath sheet out flat and cut off a strip along one short end to make one large square. Cut approximately 4 m (158 in) of 4-cm (1½-in) wide bias strips from the striped cotton fabric.

2 From the towel offcut, cut a right-angle triangle measuring about 36 cm (14 in) along the right-angled sides. Make sure that the diagonal edge runs along the woven towel edge so that you won't have to stitch a hem.

3 Place the triangle across one corner of the towel square and tack the edges in place. Use a small saucer as a template to round off each corner of the towel.

4 Make a hanging loop from a short strip of striped fabric folded in half twice lengthways. Fold the strip in half again, then tack both raw ends to the top of the hood part of the towel.

5 Join the bias strips together to make a continuous length. Now apply the binding to the outer edge of the towel (see page 11).

6 For the wash mitt, simply cut out a rectangle of towelling measuring 20 cm x 30 cm (8 in x 12 in). Fold in half matching the shortest edges. Stitch across the lower edge and up the side seam. Make a small loop from a scrap of striped fabric and tack it to the top edge. Turn the mitt to the right side then apply bias binding to the top raw edge (see page 11).

Templates

The templates supplied here list how much you need to enlarge them by to make the projects in the

book. You can make the projects to different sizes, but you should keep the proportions the same.

CLOTH BOOK (ENLARGE BY 200%)

33 cm (13 in)

CUT 6
WHITE
COTTON

BOOK
NOT TO SCALE

STRAWBERRY

LEMON

APPLE

PEAR

TREE

DAISY

TULIP

CHRISTMAS TREE

BOOKENDS
(ENLARGE BY 200%)

EAR
CUT 4

BODY
CUT 2

LAUNDRY BAG
(ENLARGE BY 200%)

CUT 3 BLUE GINGHAM

CUT 6 WHITE COTTON

MOBILE (ENLARGE BY 250%)

2 X PINK, 2 X BLUE,
2 X GREEN

6 X PINK, 6 X BLUE,
6 X GREEN

2 X PINK, 2 X BLUE,
2 X GREEN

6 X BLUE, 4 X PINK,
4 X GREEN

116 cm (46 in)

BAG
NOT TO SCALE
CUT 1 PINK

50 cm (19½ in)

BAG
NOT TO SCALE
CUT 1 BLUE

25 cm (10 in)

116 cm (46 in)

LINING
NOT TO SCALE

75 cm (30 in)

CRIB QUILT
(ENLARGE BY 200%)

CORNER
SQUARE
CUT 10 RED
POLKA DOT

CUT 6 DARK PATTERN
6 LIGHT PATTERN

STRAP
CUT 17 RED

LAMPSHADE (ENLARGE BY 200%)

WIRE INITIAL (ENLARGE BY 200%)
INSERT OTHER INITIALS AS REQUIRED

FLOOR MAT (ENLARGE BY 200%)

85 cm (33¹/₂ in)

65 cm (25¹/₂ in)

4 in (10 cm)

10 cm x 65 cm (4 in x 21¹/₂ in)

10 cm x 65 cm (4 in x 21¹/₂ in)

10 cm x 65 cm (4 in x 21¹/₂ in)

4 in (10 cm)

1 in (2.5

NOT TO SCALE
(MEASUREMENTS
APPROXIMATE)

5 cm (2 in)

FROG

DUCK

PULL-ALONG PATCH
(ENLARGE BY 200%)

FRONT LEG
CUT 2

BODY
CUT 1

HIND LEG
CUT 2

COT/BUGGY DECORATION
(ENLARGE BY 200%)

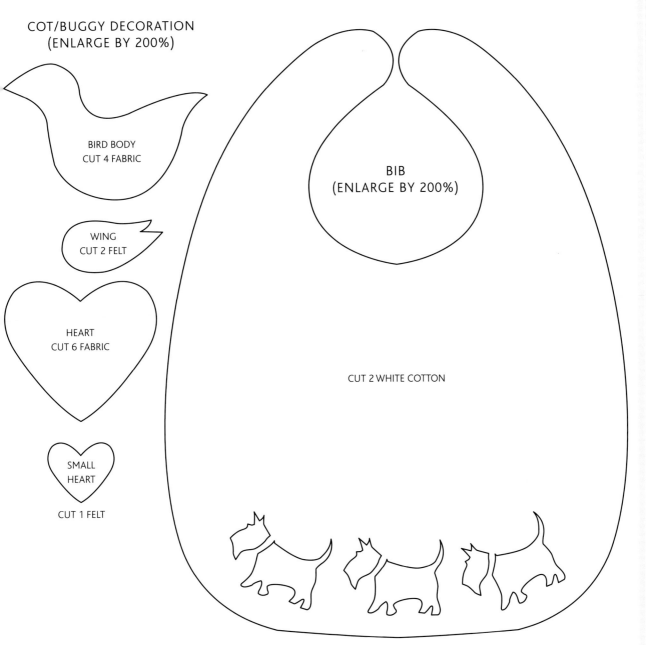

BIRD BODY
CUT 4 FABRIC

WING
CUT 2 FELT

HEART
CUT 6 FABRIC

SMALL
HEART

CUT 1 FELT

BIB
(ENLARGE BY 200%)

CUT 2 WHITE COTTON

CUSHIONS
(ENLARGE ACCORDING TO PREFERENCE)

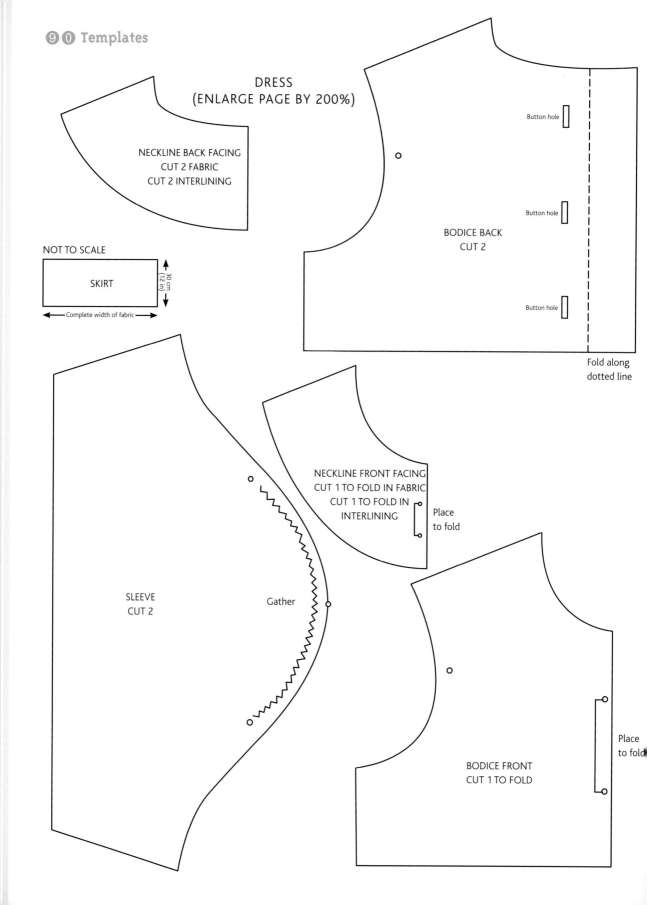

DRESS
(ENLARGE PAGE BY 200%)

NECKLINE BACK FACING
CUT 2 FABRIC
CUT 2 INTERLINING

Button hole

Button hole

BODICE BACK
CUT 2

Button hole

Fold along
dotted line

NOT TO SCALE

SKIRT

30 cm
(12 in)

Complete width of fabric

NECKLINE FRONT FACING
CUT 1 TO FOLD IN FABRIC
CUT 1 TO FOLD IN
INTERLINING

Place
to fold

SLEEVE
CUT 2

Gather

Place
to fold

BODICE FRONT
CUT 1 TO FOLD

CARDIGAN
(ENLARGE PAGE BY 200%)

BACK
CUT 1 TO FOLD IN KNITTED FABRIC
CUT 1 TO FOLD IN LINING

Place
to fold

FRONT
CUT 2 KNITTED FABRIC
CUT 2 LINING

SLEEVE
CUT 2 KNITTED FABRIC
CUT 2 LINING

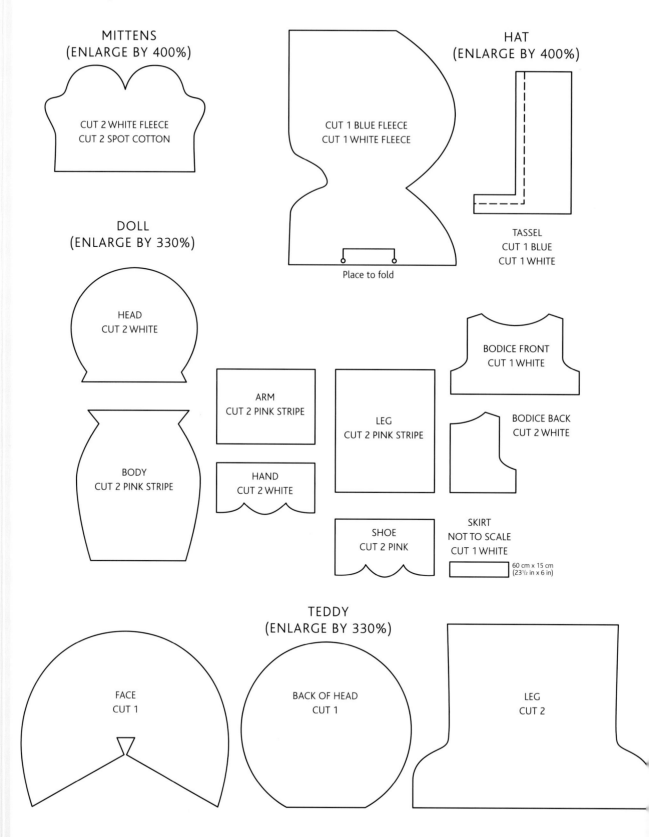

MITTENS
(ENLARGE BY 400%)

CUT 2 WHITE FLEECE
CUT 2 SPOT COTTON

HAT
(ENLARGE BY 400%)

CUT 1 BLUE FLEECE
CUT 1 WHITE FLEECE

Place to fold

TASSEL
CUT 1 BLUE
CUT 1 WHITE

DOLL
(ENLARGE BY 330%)

HEAD
CUT 2 WHITE

ARM
CUT 2 PINK STRIPE

BODICE FRONT
CUT 1 WHITE

LEG
CUT 2 PINK STRIPE

BODICE BACK
CUT 2 WHITE

BODY
CUT 2 PINK STRIPE

HAND
CUT 2 WHITE

SHOE
CUT 2 PINK

SKIRT
NOT TO SCALE
CUT 1 WHITE

60 cm x 15 cm
(23 1/2 in x 6 in)

TEDDY
(ENLARGE BY 330%)

FACE
CUT 1

BACK OF HEAD
CUT 1

LEG
CUT 2

Cut along this line front piece only   Place to fold

BEACH ROBE (ENLARGE BY 330%)

FRONT AND BACK
CUT 2

Place to hem of towel

Place to hem of towel

HOOD
CUT 1 TO FOLD

Place to fold

POCKET
CUT 1

SLEEVE – CUT 2

Place to hem of towel

MORE TEDDY (ENLARGE BY 330%)

ARM
CUT 2

SOLE OF FOOT
CUT 2

EAR
CUT 2

Pleat

Arm position

BODY
CUT 2

Arm position

NAPPY DISPENSER

Depth of nappy bag

BASE
CUT 1

Width of nappy bag

FLAP
CUT 1

Cut to fold

Circumference of nappy bag

CUT 1
IN FABRIC

2 x height of nappy bag

CHANGING BAG (ENLARGE AS SHOWN)

55 cm (22 in)

40 cm (16 in)

BAG
CUT 2 FABRIC
CUT 2 LINING

15 cm (6 in)

15 cm (6 in)

25 cm (10 in)

55 cm (22 in)

25 cm (10 in)

POCKET
CUT 1 FABRIC
CUT 1 LINING

15 cm (6 in)

15 cm (6 in)

25 cm (10 in)

HANDLES
CUT 2 FABRIC
CUT 2 LINING

TAB

4 cm (1½ in)

6 cm (2½ in)

CUT LINING

75 cm (30 in)

7 (2½

TROUSERS/DUNGAREES (ENLARGE BY 400%)

• BASE OF FASTENING TAB

TROUSERS
FRONT AND BACK
CUT 4

FRONT
CUT 1 TO FOLD IN
LINING AND FABRIC

Place to fold

BACK
CUT 1 TO FOLD IN
LINING AND FABRIC

Place to fold

FELT BOOTEES (ENLARGE BY 400%)

UPPER

CUT 2 BLUE
CUT 2 PINK

SOLE

CUT 2 BLUE

CUT 2 PINK

FLEECE COAT (ENLARGE BY 400%)

HOOD
CUT 1 LIGHT PINK
CUT 1 DARK PINK

Place to fold

Centre back seam

FRONT
CUT 2 LIGHT PINK
CUT 2 DARK PINK

SLEEVE
CUT 2 LIGHT PINK
CUT 2 DARK PINK

CUT 4
DARK
PINK

LOOP

TOGGLE

CUT 4
LIGHT PINK
CUT 4
DARK PINK

BACK
CUT 1 TO FOLD
IN LIGHT PINK
CUT 1 TO FOLD
IN DARK PINK

SOFT PLAY BLOCKS
(ENLARGE BY 400%)

STAR
CUT 2 PER
BLOCK

SQUARE
CUT 6 PER
BLOCK

POCKET TIDY
(ENLARGE BY 400%)

Top fold line

POCKET FLAP
CUT 2 IN 4 COLOURS

PADDED HANGER (ENLARGE BY 400%)

COVER

○

Index

A

appliqué 12, 16, 26, 29, 34, 48, 58, 76

B

baby's first mittens 63
bags 70, 75, 76, 81
beach robe 55
bear 42
bias binding 11, 16, 55, 56, 64, 70, 81, 82
bib 82
blocks 34
bootees 58
buggy decoration 47

C

cardigan 56
casings 10, 70, 76
changing bag 75
changing mat 78
cloth book 48
coat 66
cosy blanket 26
cot decoration 47
countersinking 13
crib quilt 16
cushions 29

D

doll 44
drawstring bag 70
dress 52
drill 13
dungarees 64

E

elephant bookends 30
embroidery stitches 12
equipment 8, 9

F

felt bootees 58
fleece coat 66
floor mat 41

G

gathering 11, 52, 64
gluing 13

H

hat 60
hems 10
hooded towel 84

J

jigsaw 13

K

keepsake memory box 22

L

lampshade 18
laundry bag 76

M

mittens 63
mobile 36

N

nappy dispenser 81

P

padded hanger 70
painting 13
pilot holes 13
plain seams 10
plywood 13
pocket tidy 25
power equipment 9, 13
pull-along Patch 38

R

Raggedy Ann doll 44

S

safety 9
screws 13
seams 10
sewing kit 9
sewing skills 10–11
soft play blocks 34
stencilling 13, 41
storage bucket 72
surface decoration 12

T

teddy 42
templates 86-95
topstitching 11, 75
trousers 64

W

wash mitt 84
wirework initials 21
woodwork 13, 22, 30, 38